This Book Was Donated to the Adaire School Library by the "Adaire Home And School Association" 1993-1995

JOURNEY THROUGH

Canada

Richard Tames

Troll Associates

Library of Congress Cataloging-in-Publication Data

Tames, Richard.
    Journey through Canada / by Richard Tames;
illustrated by Martin Camm...[et al.].
        p.   cm.
    Summary: Describes the geography, sights,
and prominent places of Canada. Includes
a chart of key facts and information on the
climate, natural resources, and people.
    ISBN 0-8167-2110-6 (lib. bdg.)
    ISBN 0-8167-2111-4 (pbk.)
    1. Canada—Juvenile literature.
[1. Canada.]   I. Camm, Martin, ill.
II. Title.
F1008.2.T36   1991
971—dc20   90-10934

Published by Troll Associates, Mahwah,
New Jersey 07430

Edited by Neil Morris

Design by James Marks
Picture research by Caroline Mitchell.
Illustrators: Martin Camm: pages 4-5, 22-23;
Mike Roffe: pages 5, 16-17, 26-27; Paul Sullivan:
page 11; Ian Thompson: pages 4-5, 24

Picture Credits: B & C Alexander pages 16-17,
17; Barnabys: page 27; Canadian High
Commission pages 8-9, 15 (bottom), 22-23, 25;
J Allan Cash pages 24-25; Cam Culbert
pages 20-21; Robert Estall pages 7 (bottom), 13, 14,
21; Hutchison: pages 10, 10-11, 29; Survival
Anglia: page 9; Richard Tames page 19; ZEFA:
cover, pages 1, 6/7, 7 (top), 12-13 (top & bottom), 15
(top), 18-19, 20, 26, 28, 30

Printed in the U.S.A.
10   9   8   7   6   5   4   3   2   1

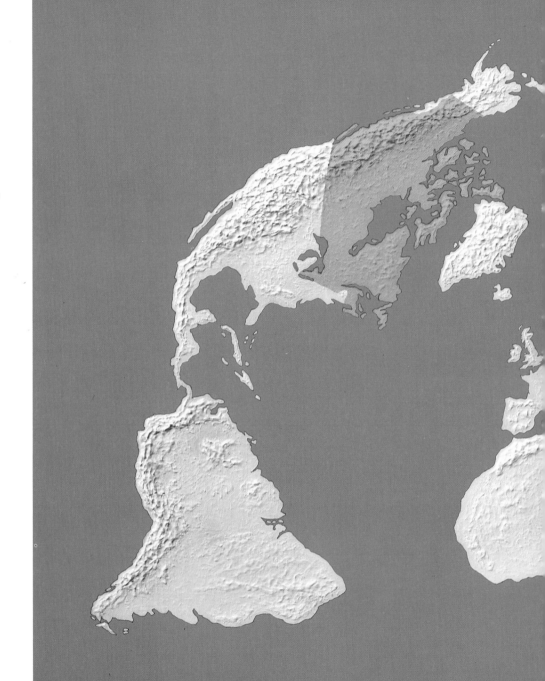

CONTENTS

Canada

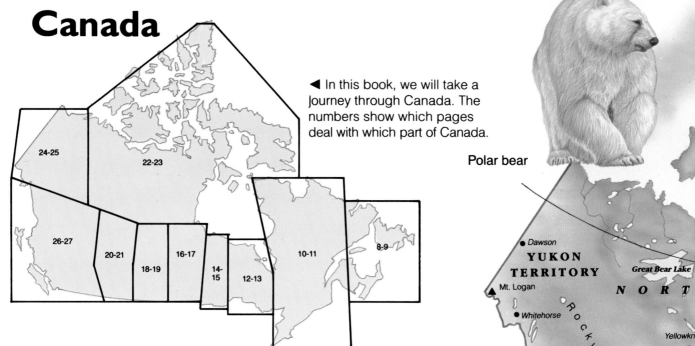

◄ In this book, we will take a journey through Canada. The numbers show which pages deal with which part of Canada.

Polar bear

Snow goose

KEY FACTS

Area: 9,971,000 sq. km (3,850,000 sq. mi.) – the second biggest country in the world

Population: 25,334,000 people

Capital: Ottawa 819,000 people in the metropolitan area

Other major cities: Toronto 3,427,000 Montreal 2,921,000 Vancouver 1,381,000

Highest mountain: Mount Logan 6,050 m (19,850 ft.)

Longest river: Mackenzie 1,770 km (1,100 mi.)

Largest lake: Lake Superior, 82,400 sq. km (31,800 sq. mi.), situated between the U.S.A. and Canada, is the largest freshwater lake in the world.

The symbol on the Canadian flag is a red maple leaf. The maple tree is common in Canada, and its leaves turn red in the fall. The Canadian national anthem is *O Canada;* the music was composed in 1880, the words were written in 1908, but it only became the national anthem in 1980.

ALERT

ELLESMERE ISLAND

BAFFIN ISLAND

ARCTIC CIRCLE

WEST T E R R I T O R I E S

A T L A N T I C

N E W F O U N D L A N D
L A B R A D O R

H u d s o n
B a y

SASKATCHEWAN

MANITOBA

Q U E B E C

O C E A N

PR. EDWARD ISL.

CAPE BRETON ISLAND

Charlottetown

St. John's

O N T A R I O

NEW
BRUNSWICK

St. Lawrence River

Quebec

Fredericton

Halifax

NOVA
SCOTIA

TRANS-CANADA HIGHWAY

Regina

Winnipeg

Lake of the Woods

Thunder Bay
Lake Superior

Montreal

OTTAWA

Toronto

Lake Huron

Hamilton

Lake Erie

Lake Ontario

Niagara Falls

Moose

Animals of Canada
Polar bears live on the ice-packed northern coasts. The snow goose is an Arctic bird. The moose is the largest member of the deer family.

Welcome to Canada

Canada is huge. It is the second largest country in the world after the U.S.S.R. It covers nearly 10 million square kilometers (4 million square miles). It takes seven hours to cross Canada by airplane. Much of Canada is covered by a great forest that spreads from the Atlantic Ocean to the Pacific Ocean. The forest is one of the largest in the world. It has deciduous and coniferous trees. There are hundreds of lakes and rivers in the forest. There may be as many as a million lakes in Canada, but no one is sure.

Early settlers gave Canada its name. It is a strange name for such a vast country. The word *kanata* in the Iroquois Indian language means "village!"

The Indians and Inuit have lived in Canada for thousands of years. The Vikings sailed across the Atlantic Ocean and settled in Newfoundland over a thousand years ago. They were the first Europeans to settle in North America. In 1497 John Cabot sailed from England and landed at St. John's. His sailors named the island "New Found Land." He named the port St. John's, as they landed on St. John's Day. Today most Canadians live along the border with the United States of America. The rest of the country has fewer people living in it.

Canada is divided into ten provinces and two territories. It is too large a country to be governed without being divided up. There are two official languages, English and French. Each province decides which is its official language.

Canada is an exciting country to visit. It has old things to see, like dinosaur bones, and new ones, like the tallest free-standing building in the world. There are many friendly people to meet, but also vast areas of beautiful countryside with no one in sight. Enjoy your journey across Canada!

▲ Mount Eisenhower, in Banff National Park, Alberta. This was the first of Canada's 35 national parks. It has forests of pine, fir, spruce, and larch.

▶ The "Prairie Provinces" of Manitoba, Saskatchewan, and Alberta form the main wheat-producing area of Canada.

▲ Blackfoot Indians lived on the Great Plains of the U.S.A. and Canada. Many now live on their own reserves in Canada. The Blackfoot were once great hunters.

The journey begins

St. John's in Newfoundland is the ideal starting point for your journey. It is the most easterly point in Canada. From there you can drive along the Trans-Canada Highway all the way to Vancouver on the west coast. The Highway is about 8,000 kilometers (5,000 miles) long and is signed by a white maple leaf on a green background.

To the north of Newfoundland province lies the Coast of Labrador. It is covered with snow for six months of the year, and is home to huge herds of caribou. Labrador is more than twice as big as the island of Newfoundland.

As you leave the island, you can take a ferry as far as Cape Breton. From there you cross a bridge to rejoin the mainland at Nova Scotia. Nova Scotia means New Scotland. The flag of Nova Scotia includes the cross of Saint Andrew, the patron saint of Scotland. The capital of Nova Scotia is Halifax. It has a large harbor, one of the few in Canada that does not freeze in winter. Fishing is a very important industry in both Newfoundland and Nova Scotia.

Prince Edward Island lies to the north of Nova Scotia. It is the smallest province in Canada, the only one not on the Trans-Canada Highway. It played an important part in Canada's history over a hundred years ago when several of Canada's leaders met at its capital, Charlottetown, to decide to join Canada's provinces into a single nation.

The white maple leaf sign will lead you to New Brunswick, the only province with both French and English as its official languages. If you leave the Highway, you will see some of the famous covered bridges. The covers protect the bridges from snow. The longest covered bridge is at Hartland and is about 265 meters (870 feet) long.

◄ The white maple leaf is the sign for the Trans-Canada Highway. This road runs across Canada, from coast to coast.

► The caribou is a large deer. Both male and female caribou have antlers. The antlers that grow over the face may be used to clear snow from mosses and lichens.

◄ These Newfoundland fishermen are drying a catch of cod. Tiny, isolated fishing villages called "outports" line the rocky, windswept coasts of Newfoundland. In the Grand Banks fishing grounds, there are huge shoals of cod, haddock, herring, mackerel, Atlantic salmon, and lobster.

Bonjour!

When you arrive in Quebec, you will see that everything around you is French. People speak French, their food is French, the signs are in French. Quebec is a French-speaking province. Its main cities are Montreal and Quebec City.

Quebec is the only walled city in North America. It has many old and famous buildings. It has become a major port on the St. Lawrence River. Its main trade was in furs, but now timber is very important. You can travel down the St. Lawrence to Montreal. Montreal is also a mixture of old and new. There are narrow cobbled streets as well as a 13-kilometer (8-mile) underground walkway of shops.

If you visit Quebec City at the beginning of February you will find it very cold, but fun. There is a Winter Carnival with competitions for ice sculpture.

An unusual way of exploring the rivers and lakes of Quebec is by raft. Many Canadians have a holiday house by a lake. Sometimes the only way to reach it is by boat or water plane, as there are often no roads through the forest. The forests are also home to black bears!

▲ There are French and English schools in Quebec. These youngsters at a French-language school are working on a group project.

▼ Logs floating beneath a bridge across the St. Maurice River. Softwood trees supply timber for pulpwood, which is used to make paper.

Ice hockey is Canada's most popular game. Every park in Montreal has an ice rink. The game is very fast and exciting. Canadians enjoy both playing and watching it. Lacrosse is another game enjoyed in Canada. It was first played by the Iroquois Indians, when two hundred people would take part. Today there are only ten or twelve on a team.

◄ Ice hockey is Canada's national sport. There are hockey leagues for young players throughout the country. The National Hockey League includes American teams. In May, nearly everyone stays at home to watch on TV the finals of the game's top trophy, the Stanley Cup. The Montreal Canadiens have won the cup more often than any other team.

Canada's capital

Ottawa was chosen as capital of Canada by Queen Victoria. It was then called Bytown, but it was renamed Ottawa. Ottawa means "a place of buying and selling." The city is built beside the Ottawa River, a tributary of the St. Lawrence. The Rideau Canal cuts right through the center of the city. During winter, people often skate along the frozen canal to their offices.

Toronto is the largest city in Canada and the capital of Ontario. Toronto means "meeting place." It was where fur traders met. Today the city is the most important business center in Canada and has the country's busiest airport. It is also the most international city in Canada with people from Europe, Asia, the Caribbean, and the United States of America.

From Toronto, you can fly to Thunder Bay on the other side of Ontario. Flying is the quickest way of traveling around Canada. Many places that would otherwise be very isolated can rely on a link by air in case of an emergency. Flying is also a wonderful way of seeing the Canadian countryside. You can see the great forest of Canada with its hundreds of rivers and lakes spread beneath you in every direction.

As you fly to Thunder Bay, you will see Lake Huron and Lake Superior. They are two of the five Great Lakes. Along the edges of the lakes are farms and steel mills. Ontario has more industry than any of the other provinces.

▶ Hamilton, south of Toronto on Lake Ontario, is Canada's steel capital. The flaming chimneys of huge steel mills dominate the bay area.

◄ The famous Niagara Falls are on the Niagara River, which flows out of Lake Erie. The Falls are on the border between Canada and the U.S.A. The Horseshoe or Canadian Falls are about 47 meters (158 feet) high. They are well worth the 90-minute drive from Toronto to see.

▼ Ottawa, Toronto, and other Ontario towns all have interesting markets. As well as fruit and vegetables, you will find bottles of maple syrup for sale. This is a sweet syrup made from the sap of the sugar maple tree.

The center of Canada

The Iroquois Indians lived in Thunder Bay and Ontario long before the Europeans. The Iroquois were farmers who would make a clearing in the forest and plant corn, sunflowers, melons, and tobacco. After about ten years they would move on to another site. The women did most of the work on the land while the men went hunting and fishing.

When you fly into Thunder Bay, the first things you notice are the huge grain elevators. All the wheat from the prairies is stored here. It is then shipped

▶ The Canadian Pacific Railway was completed in 1885. Now there are fewer trains as road and air travel become more popular.

▼ These children are enjoying their game of ice hockey on a frozen Ontario pond.

through the Great Lakes to the St. Lawrence River. Thunder Bay is in the center of Canada, but is connected to the sea by the Great Lakes and a series of waterways.

Travel by air, road, and rail are all popular in Canada. The Canadian Pacific Railway runs from Toronto to Vancouver. The railway was completed in 1885, and links eastern and western Canada. You can catch the train at Thunder Bay and travel to Winnipeg. Each train has a viewing coach with a large glass dome. You can sit high up with an excellent view of the countryside around you. This view will change dramatically during the journey, from the enormous forests and lakes of Ontario to the plains of Manitoba.

One of the sights on the way to Winnipeg is the Lake of the Woods, on the border with the U.S.A. This lake has so many inlets and peninsulas that its shoreline is longer than Lake Superior's.

▲ Grain elevators at Thunder Bay, on the shores of Lake Superior. Grain is lifted into these towers and stored there, ready for shipping down the St. Lawrence Seaway.

Gateway to the prairies

Winnipeg is the capital of Manitoba. It is the gateway to the prairies and the first of the great wheat-growing provinces. Most of the wheat that is grown here is sent abroad.

Before the Europeans came to Canada, the Blackfoot Indians hunted the buffalo that grazed on prairie grass. They used bows and arrows, so not too many animals were killed. When the Spanish explorers came to North America, they brought horses which the Indians exchanged for furs and skins. Horses became important in the hunting of buffalo. When the Europeans came with their guns, most of the herds of buffalo were wiped out.

Many people moved to Manitoba for a better life – Scots, French Canadians, farmers from Ontario and the United States, German-speaking Russians, Icelanders, Swiss, Swedes, Hungarians, and Ukrainians. Many of these groups have kept their customs and languages. Throughout the year there are ethnic festivals. The biggest is Folklorama in Winnipeg. It is a celebration and exhibition of work, culture, and cooking from all over the world.

▼ The long-distance bus system links most towns and cities in Canada.

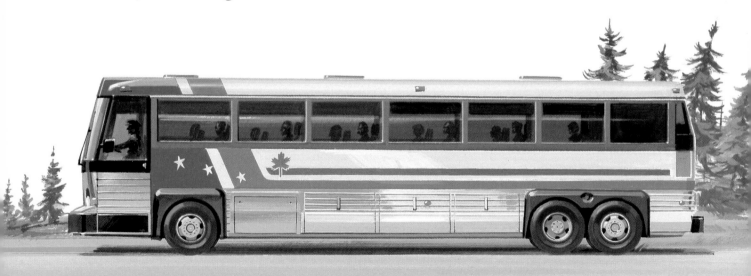

From Winnipeg you can take a bus along the Trans-Canada Highway. Buses link most towns and cities in North America, and they are a good way of seeing the countryside. For the first time on the journey west the scenery will be very different, with great plains stretching to the horizon. You could make your first stop at Brandon, where you can see the longest swinging footbridge in the whole of Canada. It is 582 footsteps across.

▲ Winnipeg was a small fur-trading village in 1870, when the province of Manitoba was created. Now it is a busy and important city, and the home of two universities.

▶ Bands of Cree Indians used to roam the great forests of the Manitoba region. The name Winnipeg comes from the Cree word meaning "muddy waters." Cree Indians lived traditionally in *wigwams*, skin or bark tents with a pole framework. Few Canadian Indians now live in the traditional way.

The home of the Mounties

Saskatchewan is sometimes called the "wheat province," as it produces much of Canada's wheat. This is despite the temperature, which can range from 45°C (113°F) in the short sunny summer to −45°C (−50°F) in the long winter.

Regina is the capital of Saskatchewan. It is the main training place of the Royal Canadian Mounted Police, or the Mounties, as they are better known. The Mounties kept order among the settlers and gold seekers in the Rocky Mountains. They also protected the Indians. In the days of the pioneers and the gold rush, Mounties patrolled on horseback. Today, they often use aircraft for their patrols. In 1969, the Mounties retired their husky dogs and sleds in favor of snowmobiles.

The Mounties have a museum in Regina. It includes the story of Sitting Bull, the Sioux Indian chief, who fled to Canada after the Battle of Little Big Horn. The last battle in Canada was in Saskatchewan in 1885 when Louis Riel, a settler of French and Indian descent, led a rebellion against the Canadian government. Louis Riel was executed in Regina after his defeat. The Canadian Pacific Railway played a vital part in stopping the rebellion as it brought troops from Ottawa by rail.

As you cross the border into Alberta, the scenery will not change a great deal. But as you approach Calgary, you will see the vast Rocky Mountains.

► The Royal Canadian Mounted Police, or Mounties, were founded in 1873. Over the years, they have gained a reputation for persistence and bravery. They are still real policemen, and have the power to enforce all national laws.

► Wheat fields stretch as far as the eye can see on the vast plains of Saskatchewan. Grain elevators stand along the road outside a village south of Regina.

Cowboys and Indians

Calgary is Canada's fastest growing city. Most of the oil and gas exploration companies working in Alberta are based there. It grew up as a cattle town. As the buffalo disappeared from the prairies, they were replaced by herds of cattle. Calgary became the center for cattle ranches and great meat-packing businesses. This period of its history is remembered during the Calgary Stampede. Every summer for ten days the city becomes a "cowtown" again with rodeo contests, chuck-wagon races, and colorful parades of cowboys, Indians, and Mounties.

Alberta's capital, Edmonton, is north of Calgary. As you travel, you pass through countryside once inhabited by dinosaurs. More dinosaur bones have been found in Alberta than anywhere else in the world. The city began as a Hudson's Bay Company fur-trading post. The Hudson's Bay Company had trading posts all over northern Canada. Today many of the shops in the north are run by the Company.

Before Europeans brought guns to the prairies, the Indians killed buffalo by stampeding them over steep cliffs. At a place called "Head-Smashed-In Buffalo Jump" there is a layer of buffalo bones four meters (13 feet) thick, the result of 5,000 years of hunting.

A journey through Canada would not be complete without a visit to the far north of the country. You can fly from Edmonton to Yellowknife. This will give you some idea of Canada's size. You will fly over vast areas of forest, lakes, and rivers with no human settlement in sight.

▶ Lake Louise is surrounded by mountains and glaciers. This is the perfect place to rent a canoe.

20

▲ The Calgary Stampede festival first took place in 1912. Most events are held in Stampede Park, including the bucking bulls contest. Calgary streets are full of life too.

▶ A snowmobile outside a Hudson's Bay store. Winter in the mountains is for skiing, snowshoeing, and snowmobiling.

The land of the midnight sun

The north of Canada has two regions called the Northwest Territories and the Yukon Territory. There are fewer than 76,000 people living in these territories. Yellowknife is the biggest city. It is named after the copper knives once made there.

The original settlers of this wilderness are often called *Eskimo*. This is an Indian word which means "eaters of raw meat." They prefer to be called *Inuit*, which in their language, Inuktitut, means "people." Other speakers of Inuktitut live in Greenland, Alaska, and Siberia.

The Inuit learned to live in harsh conditions. They depended on catching seals and whales for food, clothes, tools, tents, and weapons. Nowadays they may work as fishermen, miners, loggers, boat-builders, Mounties, nurses, or weather observers. Inuit craft goods are highly prized. They are renowned for carving "soapstone," a kind of soft, gray rock, and for prints from rock-cut blocks.

From Yellowknife you can hire an aircraft to visit an Inuit village in the Arctic Circle. You stay at the Inuit settlement, not in an igloo but in a simple house. You can talk with the Inuit to find out about life within the Arctic Circle. If you go in winter, it should be possible to go on trips with a dog team or snowmobile. However, it is not always easy to make arrangements in advance as you can never be sure of the weather.

During the summer the sun scarcely sets, but the winter days are short and dark. In the fall, winter and spring, the sky is sometimes lit up by the bright colors of the Aurora Borealis, or northern lights. Summer lasts only six weeks on Baffin Island. In July the far north knows no darkness. When it is time for bed, the sun is still shining!

▲ Walruses, seals, whales, and narwhals live in Arctic waters. Walruses live together in herds. In the fall they drift southward with the ice. Both males and females grow tusks. These can be up to 1 meter (3 feet) long. The walrus uses its tusks when fighting and digging for food.

◄ This Inuit family has hung fish up to dry. Drying preserves the fish for later use. A small number of Inuit people still live off the land. Their lives are based on hunting and fishing. Most Inuit live in a settlement for at least part of the year. Many have full-time, year-round jobs.

Gold!

Dawson City in the Yukon suddenly became big news in 1896, when gold was discovered. Until then the town had been a fur-trading center, with Russian traders from the west dealing with the Dene, the Indians of the Yukon. In 1896 George Cormack found handfuls of gold in Bonanza Creek, which flows into the Klondike River. As soon as the news spread, thousands of people set off to search for gold. The problem was that Dawson City was not easy to reach. Thousands of people never got to the Yukon, and many were turned back by the Mounties if they did not have a year's supply of food with them. Many who did make it to Dawson City never found gold.

Five years later the rush was over. Dawson City then had a population of 80,000. Now about 700 people live there. However, mining for lead, silver, zinc, and even gold is still important in the Yukon.

From Dawson City you can drive along the Top of the World Highway through the beautiful Rockies.

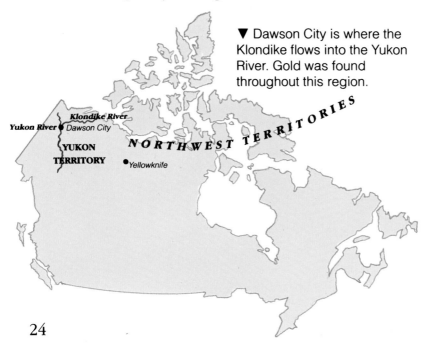

▼ Dawson City is where the Klondike flows into the Yukon River. Gold was found throughout this region.

Beside the road you can see the log cabins where the gold seekers lived. Whenever you drive in the Yukon, you must be sure your car is in good order, that you have good maps, and that you check the weather conditions. In winter you must take some food, matches for a fire, heavy blankets, and shovels in case you break down and are snowed in.

You can take a ferry from Skagway along the Inside Passage, down the coast of British Columbia to Vancouver. This is a rather easier journey!

◄ The main shaft building of a gold mine at Yellowknife, Northwest Territories. Tunnels are blasted to reach the rock that contains gold. The rock is then crushed so that the ore can be treated.

▲ Gold prospectors usually "pan" gold. They wash gravel with water in a pan. When the gravel is washed away, the heavier gold is left. This is a lengthy process, and not always successful!

The end of the journey

Vancouver in British Columbia is a harbor city ringed by snow-capped mountains. The climate in Vancouver is generally mild all year long. Many older people from the colder eastern provinces of Canada retire to British Columbia to enjoy the mild weather.

Vancouver has a large "Chinatown," where the signs are in Chinese and the shops sell Chinese goods. Many Chinese people helped to build the Canadian Pacific Railway, which ends at Vancouver. British Columbia also traded with China for silk and tea. Since the Panama Canal opened in 1915 and linked British Columbia with the Atlantic Ocean, Vancouver has been Canada's largest port.

You can go up forty floors in the elevator of the Harbor Center block for the best views of the city. From there you can see Stanley Park, the world's largest town park. You can rent roller skates and skate around it. In the Park you will see totem poles carved by the Indians of British Columbia.

► Indian totem poles in Stanley Park, Vancouver. Totem poles were carved and painted by Indian tribes who lived near the northwest Pacific coast. Some were used as grave memorials for chiefs. Others showed family emblems, usually animals taken from ancient legends.

▲ Vancouver's "Chinatown" is a lively community of people of Chinese descent. The restaurants serve wonderful food. There is a classical Chinese garden, and a Chinese-language newspaper called *The Chinese Times*.

British Columbia has something of all the other provinces of Canada – forestry, mining, farming, fishing, and spectacular scenery. Our journey comes to an end here on the Pacific coast. We have traveled all the way from the Atlantic Ocean, across the vast and beautiful country of Canada.

▼ A glacier in north British Columbia. A glacier is a mass of ice so thick that it moves by the force of gravity and the pressure of its own weight.

Fact file

Climate

In central and eastern Canada it is very hot in summer and very cold in winter. Canada's highest recorded temperature was in Midale, Saskatchewan, at 45°C (113°F). The lowest temperature was recorded at Snag in the Northwest Territories at −63°C (−81°F). The heaviest seasonal snowfall occurred at Revelstoke, British Columbia, in the winter of 1971/72, at 24.5 m (80 ft.). The highest wind speed (for an hour) was at Cape Hopes Advance, Quebec, at 203 km.p.h (127 m.p.h.). The foggiest place in Canada is Grand Bank in Newfoundland.

Forests

Large areas of Canada are covered by forests. There are more than 14.5 hectares (36 acres) of forest for every person in the country. Canada is the world's largest exporter of pulpwood and paper, and the third biggest softwood producer after the U.S.S.R. and the U.S.A. Canada's tallest trees are on Vancouver Island. They are Douglas firs that grow to an average height of 83 m (272 ft.). They can be as big as 9 m (30 ft.) around the base of the trunk.

▼ The St. Lawrence River at Quebec.

Lakes

Canada probably has more lakes than any other country in the world. Four of the Great Lakes – Superior, Huron, Erie, and Ontario – are divided by the border between Canada and the U.S.A. They are connected by waterways, along with Lake Michigan in the U.S.A., and discharge through the St. Lawrence into the Atlantic Ocean. There is a lake in Manitoba called Pekwachnamaykoskwaskwaypinwanik Lake, the longest place-name in the country.

Farming

The average Canadian farmer produces enough each year to feed 55 people. The world's largest wheatfield was sown in 1951 near Lethbridge in Alberta and covered 14,000 hectares (35,000 acres). Canada is the world's second largest producer of wheat after the U.S.S.R.

Natural resources

Canada is extremely rich in natural minerals. It is the world's largest producer of uranium, the second largest producer of potash and zinc, and the third largest producer of gold. The Athabasca Tar Sands in Alberta probably contain more than half the world's oil reserves. The oil pipeline from nearby Edmonton is the largest in the world. It runs across Canada to Buffalo, NY, U.S.A., a distance of 2,856 km (1,775 mi.).

▶ Black bears are protected by law.

Bears

In the Canadian forests the biggest animals you will find are bears, deer, and moose. Grizzly bears live in the Rocky Mountains. They are not normally fierce, but they can be dangerous if they are made angry. An injured male, or a female separated from her cubs, may attack people. Grizzlies eat both meat and plants. Black bears live all over Canada. Although they are called black, their fur can be dark brown or a blue-black color. Years ago many bears were shot for their fur, but now they are protected by law. There are many black bears in national parks, where their numbers are growing. Polar bears live in the north of Canada, prowling among the ice floes.

The Arctic seas

Above the Arctic Circle, seals, walruses, and whales live in the Arctic Ocean. The blue whale lives in the northern seas of Canada. It is the largest living animal. It can be over 30 m (100 ft.) long and weigh 160 tons.

Most northerly settlement

The most northerly settlement in the world is the weather station at Alert, in the Northwest Territories on the northern tip of Ellesmere Island. It is 800 km (500 mi.) from the North Pole, and is closer to Moscow than to Montreal.

High tide

Canada has the world's highest tides, at the Bay of Fundy in Nova Scotia. The average rise and fall is 14 m (46 ft.). The world's strongest currents are the Nakwakto Rapids in British Columbia. They flow at 30 km.p.h. (19 m.p.h.)

Peoples

About 40 per cent of Canadians are of British origin, and 30 per cent are of French origin. A little over 1 per cent are native Canadian Indians, and a little under 1 per cent are Métis, descended from Indian and French people. The rest are people who came from other countries all over the world.

Canadian money

The unit of currency is the Canadian dollar, which is made up of 100 cents.

The two languages of Canada

Canada is one nation with two official languages: English and French. Say it in French!

good morning	bonjour
goodbye	adieu
please	s'il vous plaît
thank you	merci

Tallest tower

The world's tallest freestanding structure is the Canadian National Tower, Toronto. It is 555 m (1,822 ft.) high. A restaurant revolves in the Sky Pod 348 m (1,140 ft.) above ground. From here you can see hills 120 km (75 mi.) away. Lightning strikes the tower 200 times a year.

▼ The Canadian National Tower, Toronto.

B.C.	Time chart		
15,000- 10,000	The first Inuit begin to spread into the Arctic from Asia.	1793	Scottish explorer Alexander Mackenzie crosses the Rockies to reach the Pacific.
A.D.		1812	War between British Canadians and the U.S.A.
1000	Viking settlement at L'Anse aux Meadows.	1837	Rebellions calling for more self-government.
1497	Italian explorer John Cabot discovers Canada's east coast.	1841	Reunion of Upper and Lower Canada.
1504	St. John's established as a shore base for English fishermen.	1867	British North America Act creates a confederation of Lower Canada, Upper Canada, Nova Scotia, and New Brunswick.
1534	Jacques Cartier discovers St. Lawrence River and claims Canada for France.	1869	Louis Riel's first rebellion against federal government authority on behalf of Métis and Indians.
1583	Sir Humphrey Gilbert proclaims Newfoundland to be British.	1870	Province of Manitoba created.
1604	French establish first permanent settlement in North America at Port Royal, Nova Scotia.	1871	British Columbia joins confederation.
1610	English explorer Henry Hudson discovers Hudson Bay.	1873	Prince Edward Island joins confederation.
1663	French declare "New France" a royal colony.	1885	Canadian Pacific Railway completed. Second rebellion and execution of Louis Riel.
1713	Treaty of Utrecht gives England Acadia, Hudson Bay area, and Newfoundland.	1896	Klondike gold rush.
1759	General James Wolfe captures Quebec for England.	1905	Alberta and Saskatchewan created from part of the Northwest Territories.
1763	Treaty of Paris grants all French territory in Canada to Britain.	1931	Statute of Westminster recognizes full independence of Dominion of Canada.
1774	Quebec Act protects French customs and religion.	1949	Newfoundland joins confederation.
1775- 1783	About 40,000 Loyalists flee from the Revolutionary War in America to settle in Canada.	1959	St. Lawrence Seaway opened.
		1965	Canada adopts maple leaf flag.
1778	Captain James Cook explores Vancouver Island.	1976	Summer Olympic Games held in Montreal.
1791	Canada divided into French-speaking Lower Canada and English-speaking Upper Canada.	1982	New constitution replaces British North America Act.
		1988	Winter Olympics held in Calgary.

Index